An opin

CN00695163

WEIRD LONDON

Written by
TOM HOWELLS

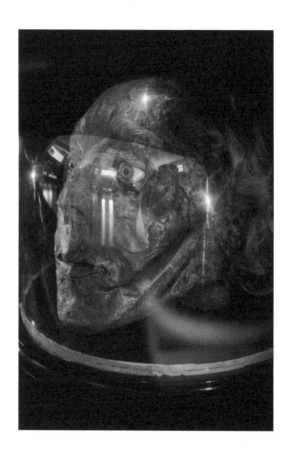

Jeremy Bentham's Auto-Icon (no. 5)

Although a weird name, Freakscene is not in this book, but we want to take you there for dinner, as a christmas present. Please share evening dates you can do. -xx -

INFORMATION IS DEAD.
LONG LIVE OPINION.

This might be a weird thing to say but guidebooks are essentially pointless. Too often, they are, like Jeremy Bentham's head (opposite), out of date and rather putrified. And why buy one when all the information you want is free online?

Well – and even more weirdly – this guidebook is not about information. It's about opinion. It's a short and sweet list of the places you *have* to see, so you don't need to do any research. And in a city known for it's touristic gloss, we thought it fun to choose the absolute weirdest stuff (good weird, not bad weird) that will reveal this city in a new and ever-so-strange light.

It might even make your head spin.

Martin
Hoxton Mini Press

London Loo Tours (no.36)
Opposite: Lady Dinah's Cat Emporium (no.18)

God's Own Junkyard (no.15)

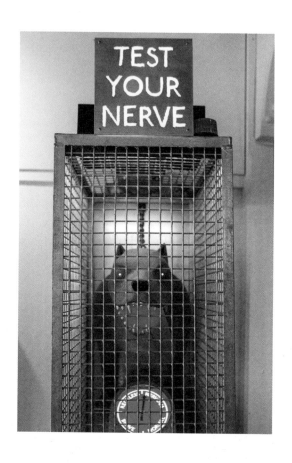

Novelty Automation (no.1)
Opposite: Neon Naked Life Drawing (no.14)

WHAT MAKES WEIRD?

The 'weird' is an amorphous thing. It's normally envisioned as the strange, unnatural or unexpected, but the late cultural theorist Mark Fisher honed in more forensically in his 2016 book *The Weird and the Eerie*, defining it as '... that which does not belong. The weird brings to the familiar something which ordinarily lies beyond it.'

I was a somewhat esoterically minded child, preoccupied with phantoms (especially those in Usborne's *World of the Unknown: Ghosts*, abject nightmare material for an '80s kid), standing stones, lost cities, cryptids, timeslips and other elements of the near-unknown. A latent fascination with the weird permeated my adult life, not least when I moved to London.

London is a relentlessly crackers place, suffused with oddball history, arcane tradition and a hyper-diverse cultural profile that, at times, doesn't so much tiptoe around wanton eccentricity as ride roughshod through it. Even after 20 years here, barely a week passes without discovering something newly perturbing, profound or Pythonesque around town.

Enter *An Opinionated Guide to Weird London*. The remit is twofold. First, it's a practical handbook to London's most perplexing points of interest and hidden corners: from locations of macabre, folkloric and occult interest to maniacal architecture and artworks, abstruse emporia, recherché restaurants and other blink-and-you'll-miss-them spots of unnerving, amusing and plain unusual intrigue. If you feel you've experienced everything the city has to offer, well... I'd wager you're mistaken, and this pocket-sized gazetteer will provide a partial roadmap to finding the rest.

But it's also an illuminating armchair resource. Very little in this book was conceived with surface-level goofiness as a USP. In fact, almost every entry offers a window into a particular socio-cultural mindset that's only become outré with the passing of time: from Victorian pet cemeteries to thousand-year sound installations, putrefying radical philosophers to suburban cave networks, riverside gibbets to towering stinkpipes, memorials to vanquished fatbergs and a ruff-sporting puss in a dusty lawyer's pub. Admirable exceptions abound (I'm looking at you, Novelty Automation), but London's oddest locales are often more bizarre for playing things entirely straight – laden with very real, and occasionally heartfelt, subtext.

The more you look, the more Fisher's definition of the weird evokes the beautiful, unsettling sense of the odd and uncanny that spreads, tendril-like, through the city. With any luck, this book will help one see it all a little more lucidly.

Tom Howells
London, 2024

Tom Howells is a London-based journalist and editor, and has written for Vogue, the Financial Times, Wallpaper*, Time Out *and* The Guardian, *among others. He's happiest when wandering the neolithic barrows and stones of the Isle of Wight, and once got locked in Carisbrooke Castle.*

BEST FOR...

Nocturnal outings

Genius arcade Novelty Automation (no.1) is all the more uproarious on the first Thursday of the month – when it's open late and (crucially) has a makeshift bar. Or take a tour of Dennis Severs' House (no.17) by candlelight; its 'living still life' vibe takes on the full chiaroscuro effect after dark.

Retail therapy

Donlon Books (no.21) is a veritable trove of countercultural reading material, while Treadwell's (no.6) groans with practical tomes on fringe spiritualism and the occult. Boutique-cum-trance-cave Cyberdog (no.55) is a perennially future-facing resource for dayglo club and fetish wear.

The great outdoors

Take an amble along the bucolic Parkland Walk in north London, noting the eldritch Spriggan (no.53) sculpture said to have inspired a Stephen King story. Or soak up the sylvan sprawl of Sydenham Hill Woods (no.29), home to a tumbledown abbey folly and an eerie railway tunnel with a chilling urban legend.

Architectural follies

Whatever your *Grand Designs* aspirations, you've nothing on the wackadoodle postmodern mores of Charles Jencks' Cosmic House (no.46). Over in Twickenham, the wildly crenellated

Strawberry Hill House (no.31) was ground zero for both the Gothic Revival *and* the shuddering literary genre.

Historical enlightenment

An organised mudlark (no.32) is the perfect way to search for treasure along the Thames's muddy banks. For deep-dives of a more mysterious bent, there's nowhere more enlightening than the London Fortean Society's (no.22) rationality-based lectures on occult, paranormal and pseudoscientific topics.

Family-friendly frolics

Children, the weird little savages, adore the monstrous Darwinian appeal of the prehistoric eras – so a loop of the Crystal Palace dinosaurs (no.30) is a no-brainer. They'll also love Hoxton Street Monster Supplies (no.52): a magical repository of repulsive edible objects with a lovely literary subtext.

Stuffing your face

Purveyor of perfectly passé dishes, Oslo Court (no.58) is a time-warp, pastel-hued gem. Equally retro – but much noisier – is Tiroler Hut (no.41), an Austro-Alpine schnitzel'n'spätzle joint with a mellifluous cowbell show.

Getting crafty

Ever had the itch to position a dead rodent in uncanny human poses? Then Park Avenue Studios' (no.56) taxidermy workshops are for you. Lurid in a different way is Neon Naked Life Drawing (no.14): nude bods, slathered in UV body paints, respectfully immortalised on paper by the paying public.

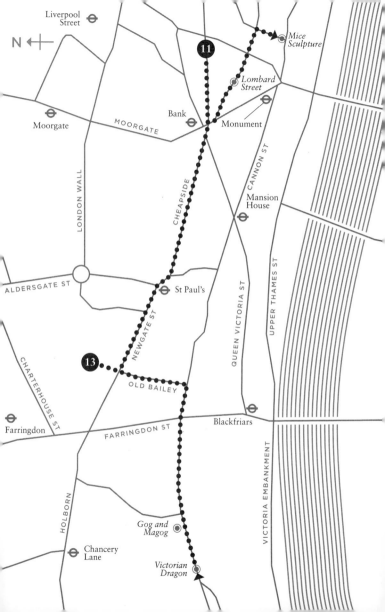

N ←

Liverpool Street

11

Mice Sculpture

Lombard Street

Bank

Monument

MOORGATE

Moorgate

CANNON ST

Mansion House

LONDON WALL

CHEAPSIDE

St Paul's

ALDERSGATE ST

NEWGATE ST

QUEEN VICTORIA ST

UPPER THAMES ST

13

OLD BAILEY

CHARTERHOUSE ST

Farringdon

FARRINGDON ST

Blackfriars

VICTORIA EMBANKMENT

HOLBORN

Gog and Magog

Chancery Lane

Victorian Dragon

LOOK UP IN THE CITY

Begin at the western end of Fleet Street: a *plinth-top Victorian dragon** – wings spread, gnashers bared – demarks the historic gates to the City. Head east and you'll spot *Gog and Magog**, two automaton giants positioned high on the church of St Dunstan-in-the-West, overlooking the first public clock in London with a minute hand. Turn towards St Paul's, swerving left up Old Bailey and over to West Smithfiled, to find the gilded remembrance to the Great Fire in the form of the gluttonous *Golden Boy of Pye Corner* ⓭. From here, walk east to Cornhill – with its looming trio of lofty *Cornhill Devils* ⑪ – before hitting parallel *Lombard Street**. Huge pictorial business signs first appeared in this goldsmithing hub in the early 18th century, becoming so extravagantly weighty that they'd occasionally pull shop frontages crashing onto the road. Four facsimiles remain: a cricket, a cat playing a fiddle, a tousled Charles II and an anchor. Finally, zip east to Fenchurch Street, and down Philpot Lane to *London's teeniest public sculpture**: two mice gorging on a hunk of cheese, above the entrance to chop shop Blacklock.

Walking time: 40 minutes, 2.4 miles
Total time with stops: 70 minutes
*Not in guidebook: more info online

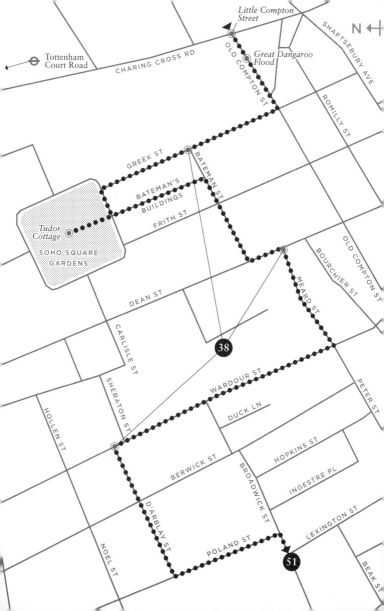

WALK 2
AMBLE AROUND SOHO

Commence, carefully, in the middle of Charing Cross road: opposite the Coach & Horses pub there's a grate on a traffic island, through which you can peek the subterranean tracts of the former *Little Compton Street**: a slum bulldozed in the late 1700s, its signage now reinstalled in this old utility subway. Spitting distance west, above Bar Termini, is a plaque marking the *'Great Dangaroo Flood'**: a fictitious natural disaster of the (also fake) 'En'kymhuirian' era, installed by Eames Demetrios as part of a 140-site art project. Turn right up Greek Street to Soho Square; its ersatz *Tudor cottage** is actually the modern entrance to an electricity substation, built in the 1920s in the style of the Tudorbethan gardener's hut that had been on this spot in the 1870s. Hunt for a few of the *Soho Noses* **38** by wending your way west-ish through Bateman, Dean and D'Arblay Streets, before zipping left down Poland Street and finishing up at the commemorative *Broad Street Cholera Pump* **51**, where Dr John Snow stemmed a cholera outbreak – before toasting the big man at his namesake pub.

Walking time: 10 minutes, 0.7 miles
Total time with stops: 1 hour
*Not in guidebook: more info online

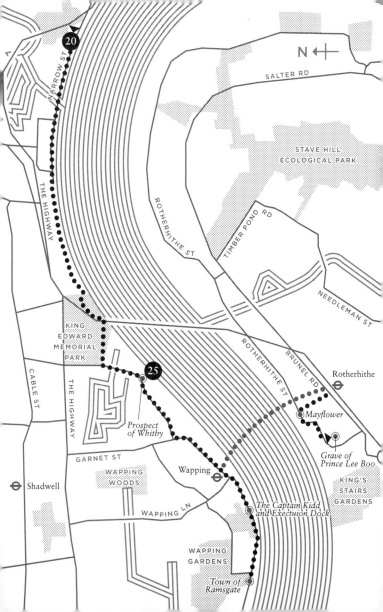

N

SALTER RD

STAVE HILL
ECOLOGICAL PARK

20

NARROW ST

THE HIGHWAY

ROTHERHITHE ST

TIMBER POND RD

NEEDLEMAN ST

BRUNEL RD

ROTHERHITHE ST

Rotherhithe

KING
EDWARD
MEMORIAL
PARK

CABLE ST

THE HIGHWAY

25

Prospect
of Whitby

Mayflower

Grave of
Prince Lee Boo

KING'S
STAIRS
GARDENS

GARNET ST

Shadwell

WAPPING
WOODS

Wapping

WAPPING LN

The Captain Kidd
and Exectuion Dock

WAPPING
GARDENS

Town of
Ramsgate

DOCKLAND DRINKING DENS

Start your crawl at *The Grapes* **20**: Ian McKellan's wood-panelled bolthole. Ambling west down the Thames Path brings you to the *Prospect of Whitby** and its replica riverside gallows **25**; ten minutes more to *The Captain Kidd**, named after the infamous privateer and alleged pirate, who was strung up (twice, as the rope snapped on first attempt) at the original *Execution Dock* **25**, down a stairway to the side of the nearby *Town of Ramsgate**. Climb back up the steps and into the bar, where the infamous Judge Jeffreys – who presided over the Bloody Assizes, trials that saw hundreds of anti-royalist rebels sentenced to death after the Monmouth Rebellion of 1685 – was apprehended, despite having shaved his capacious, trademark eyebrows off. Hop on the Overground at Wapping and go one stop south to Rotherhithe, where you can duck into the *Mayflower** (since the 1800s, the only pub in the country licensed to sell postage stamps). Chug one for the road before stumbling to St Mary's Church opposite, paying your respects at the *grave of Prince Lee Boo** – an inaugural Pacific Island visitor to Britain and a brief fixture on London's 18th-century social scene.

Walking time: 45 minutes, 2 miles
Total time with stops: 4 hours
**Not in guidebook: more info online*

1
NOVELTY AUTOMATION

Bizarre arcade of DIY automata

The irreverent fiefdom of polymath engineer/ inventor/cartoonist Tim Hunkin, this is an amusement arcade like no other. Hunkin's collection of homemade and satirical automata are truly, ecstatically odd. Where else can one present an object to a lizard-tongued effigy of former Tate boss Nicholas Serota, who'll deem it 'art' or not? Successfully direct a collection cart around an Amazon-style fulfilment centre to earn a valuable zero-hours contract? Receive essential romantic advice from Barry White on his telephone 'Love Line'; fight over the family home in a competitive divorce simulator; or test their nerve by sticking a hand in the cage of a slavering hound, with real slobber? Nowhere, that's where.

1a Princeton Street, WC1R 4AY
Nearest station: Holborn
novelty-automation.com

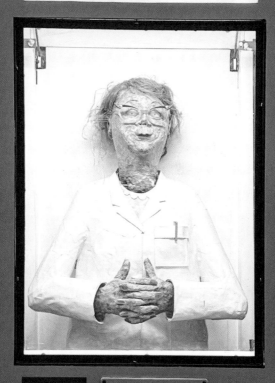

CHIROPODIST

INSTRUCTIONS

1 REMOVE SHOE, BUT NOT
  SOCK, FROM FOOT TO BE
  TREATED

2 POSITION FOOT IN
  TREATMENT BAY

3 INSERT COIN IN SLOT

2

SARASTRO

Ostentatiously operatic eatery

A wildly chintzy, evergreen institution on Drury Lane (opened in 1996 by charismatic local restaurateur Richard Niazi, aka the 'King of Covent Garden'), Sarastro is a maximalist paean to a distant age of operatic theatre. Named after a character in Mozart's *Magic Flute*, it's as flamboyant outside (flowers; foliage; palpably camp signage featuring gilded relief cherubs) as it is inside, festooned with theatrical props, golden furnishings, mounted opera boxes and, in the loos, a bevy of priapic artwork. It's not simply a feast for the eyes – as well as a rousing soundtrack of classical and operatic bangers, the fulsome menu of Mediterranean and Turkish plates has more than contributed to its long lifespan.

126 Drury Lane, WC2B 5SU
Nearest station: Temple
sarastro-restaurant.com

3

DANS LE NOIR?

A pitch-black taste explosion

Dans le Noir? is a literal feast for the senses. Some of them, anyway: the whole point of this Clerkenwell stalwart is to eat and drink in utter darkness, guided and served by blind or visually impaired staff. The MO, you see (or not), is that this vein of sensory deprivation recalibrates the way we perceive flavour and texture – a notion deployed across the 'surprise' menus of global dishes and wines, the elements of which are only revealed after you've finished scoffing. Communal dining in pitch black brings its own wine-sloshing, lap-sitting hazards – not for nothing was it the setting of a pivotal meet-cute in Richard Curtis's workaday time-travel romcom *About Time*. Best not wear white.

69–73 St John Street, ec1m 4nj
Nearest station: Farringdon
london.danslenoir.com

4

GRANT MUSEUM
OF ZOOLOGY

Academic menagerie of clapped-out creatures

This stomach-churning archive was founded in 1828 by Robert Edmond Grant, then a lauded bigwig in the world of sponges, sea slugs and molluscs. Arriving in London as UCL's first Professor of Zoology and Comparative Anatomy, he had no teaching specimens – so began to amass what would become this macabre menagerie of 68,000-ish critters preserved behind glass, floating in formaldehyde, pinned to boards and so on. It's a diverse inventory: dodo bones, the world's rarest skeleton (a kind of zebra called a 'quagga'), cleaved heads, pickled brains, an entire wall of expired mice and, most outré of all, a jar stuffed full of velvety moles. Attenborough's got nothing on this.

Rockefeller Building, 21 University Street, WC1E 6DE
Nearest stations: Warren Street, Euston Square
ucl.ac.uk/culture/grant-museum-zoology

5

JEREMY BENTHAM'S AUTO-ICON

Headless corpse of a revolutionary philosopher

Radical thinker, social reformer, founder of utilitarianism and London's most infamous publicly displayed corpse? That's Jezza Bentham who, despite dying in 1832, still sits in a glass case in the atrium of UCL's Student Centre, as per the crackers request of his will. The waxy pallor of the face is ersatz; the restoration of the real head went awry, rendering it hideous, so an artificial replacement was fashioned. The original was once displayed in a box atop the icon but, after several dubious student thefts (ransomed by rivals from KCL; used for football practice; discovered in a luggage locker at Aberdeen station), it's long been in safe storage in the Archaeology department.

27–28 Gordon Square, WC1H 0AH
Nearest station: Euston Square
ucl.ac.uk/bentham-project/
about-jeremy-bentham/auto-icon

Jeremy Bentham
(1748 – 1832)

The 'auto-icon' of philosopher and reformer Jeremy Bentham, whose educational ideas influenced the founding and development of UCL.

Bentham was a radical thinker who developed the influential doctrine of utilitarianism — that an action is right if it increases happiness — as a critical standard to judge laws, institutions and practices.

Bentham held original views on his own death. His will instructed that his corpse be dissected to benefit medical science, then preserved as the 'auto-icon' — or 'self-image' — you see here. This case holds Bentham's skeleton, which is padded, clothed and topped with a wax head.

6

TREADWELL'S BOOKS

Pan-magical bookstore with ritual supplies

In the shadow of Senate House library (an Art Deco masterpiece in its own right), Treadwell's is an arcane book depository packed with more esoteric literature than you can shake a dowsing stick at. In need of a guide to the liminal rites of the goddess Hekate? An insightful biography of arch-occultist and Thelemic bigwig Aleister 'The Beast' Crowley? Practical and theoretical guides to sex magic, talismans, grimoire, herbalism, voodoo, hoodoo, freemasonry, scrying and 'psychic self-defence'? All covered. They also hold tarot readings, a bevy of metaphysical classes and a revered lecture series on magical topics from both the ethical right-hand and more shadowy left-hand paths of spiritualism.

33 Store Street, WC1E 7BS
Nearest station: Goodge Street
treadwells-london.com

7

THE SEVEN STARS

Lilliputian lawyers' pub with a dapper mascot

Sat in the shadow of Fleet Street's Royal Courts of Justice, The Seven Stars is the City's most idiosyncratic pub. One of London's oldest boozers (supposedly opened in 1602), this dinky, clattery, wood-panelled and lace-curtained bolthole – buzzing with convivial muttering – is strewn with dusty legal ephemera, taxidermy, skull-filled Curiosity Cabinets and retro cinema paraphernalia. The beer is grand, the home-cooked fare comforting and the seating scant – not least as one chair is permanently hogged by The General: the Stars' resident cat, usually found sporting a rumpled Elizabethan ruff. Order at the bar.

53 Carey Street, WC2A 3QS
Nearest station: Chancery Lane
thesevenstars1602.co.uk

8

HAUNTED UNDERGROUND STATIONS

Skin-prickling hijinks on the Tube

London's Tube network is palpably brimming with spirits. There's a figure in opera garb at Covent Garden: the actor William Terriss, murdered by a fellow thesp in 1897 outside the Adelphi, now occasionally seen by engineers and the public come sundown. Myriad drivers at Elephant & Castle have spotted a woman entering their train but never leaving again, her presence accompanied by slamming doors and rattling footsteps. And, as the night's final carriage approaches, the lingering screams of a young girl can be heard at Farringdon, starved and murdered by the 18th-century hatmaker to whom she was apprenticed. A heady proportion more have their own shuddering tales.

Stations: Covent Garden,
Elephant & Castle, Farringdon

9

LONDON GHOST WALKS

Theatrically spooky strolls around the City

Obsessed with the City's shadowy, paranormal history, Richard Jones inaugurated his eerie urban excursions way back in 1982. His Saturday night Alleyways and Shadows tour has been a fixture ever since: commencing at Bank station and schlepping around a cursed network of backstreets (brimming with malevolent and tormented spectres), taking in the hostelry where Francis Dashwood founded his paganistic 18th-century Hellfire Club, Scrooge's counting house from *A Christmas Carol* and a lonely churchyard chamber, the occupant of which can supposedly be spurred into ghastly life with a 'ritual of the raising'. A marvellous melding of meticulous research and good old-fashioned yarning.

Princes Street, EC3V 3LA
Nearest station: Bank
london-ghost-tour.com

10

HAND OF SAINT ETHELDREDA

Desiccated mitt of a long-deceased nun

Etheldreda was a Saxon Fenland princess, who sacked off her regal trappings to become a nun in Ely, Suffolk. In 679, she croaked from a tumour on the neck – supposed divine retribution for flouncing around in necklaces – and was buried in a common grave. Fifteen years on, when her body was exhumed for an upgraded casket, it was found 'incorrupted': her neck healed and her shroud box-fresh. When she was *still* rot-free after being dug up again by the Normans, 'saint' status was confirmed. This 1250 church was built as a hangout for Ely's bishops and boasts a reverent relic in the form of Etheldreda's still putrefaction-free paw, locked away in a jewelled casket by the altar.

14 Ely Place, EC1N 6RY
Nearest station: Chancery Lane
stetheldreda.co.uk

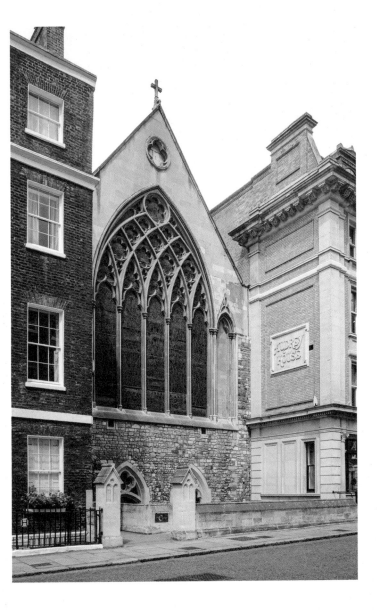

11

CORNHILL DEVILS

Trio of demons peering down from on high

A lesson in not hacking off your local architect, these three infernal icons – rendered in terracotta and perched on the gable, corner column and top window of the City's 44–45 Cornhill building – are said to have been installed after initial construction was stymied by a persnickety Victorian priest. He complained that the structure encroached onto parish land and insisted that the design be overhauled. The put-out architect, Ernest Augustus Runtz, thus installed his diabolical cohort as a heretical 'get bent' – even, apocryphally, giving one of them the face of the vicar. Either way, they remain a disquieting impish presence above the thronging City streets.

54–55 Cornhill, EC3V 3PD
Nearest station: Bank

12

HUNTERIAN MUSEUM

Stomach-churning temple to surgical history

The sprawling collections of the titular 18th-century anatomist and surgeon John Hunter isn't a place to visit before lunch. Hunter's collection of 14,000 anatomical specimens (that is to say, a *lot* of once-living things in formaldehyde) was bought by the British government in 1799, and entrusted to the Royal College of Surgeons, where it remains today. Many were lost in the Blitz, but the museum still holds 3,000 anatomical preparations (from walrus foetuses and human noses to salmon rectums, bisected crocodiles and scores of teeth), instruments, models, paintings and equipment related to the visceral art of surgery through the ages. A truly cutting-edge day out.

The Royal College of Surgeons of England,
38–43 Lincoln's Inn Fields, WC2A 3PE
Nearest station: Holborn
hunterianmuseum.org

13

GOLDEN BOY
OF PYE CORNER

Moralising memorial to the biggest blaze

The 1666 Great Fire of London famously started at Pudding Lane, but the conflagration eventually puffed out at Pye Corner, where Cock Lane and Giltspur Street meet opposite Barts Hospital. Then the site of the Fortune of War pub (beloved of resurrectionist body snatchers), the location was marked with the installation of this gleaming, nude little figure. A Papist plot was once blamed for the blaze, but an inscription below the boy implies a more epicurean origin – 'This boy is in Memory Put up for the late Fire of London, Occasion'd by the Sin of Gluttony, 1666' – while a second text makes note of his 'prodigiously fat' appearance. Wanton body-shaming: he's not even that chubby.

Giltspur Street, ECIA 9DD
Nearest stations: Farringdon, Barbican

This Boy is
in Memmory Put up
for the late FIRE of
LONDON
Occasion'd by the
Sin of Gluttony
1666

14

NEON NAKED LIFE DRAWING

Classic nude scribbling with a fluoro flourish

Life drawing is a ubiquitous activity around creatively liberated London these days. Stepping things up a notch is artist and avant garde fashionista Jylle Navarro. Her dazzling, LED/UV-soaked take on the form sees the fleshy subject daubed in reactive body paint and wackadoodle fluorescent accessories, affording new landscapes of mind-bending colour and texture – a psychedelic mish-mash of high art, Leigh Bowery-style threads and a psytrance chillout room. Materials are supplied, and alternative mark-making techniques (such as pointillism, auto-drawing and continuous line) are encouraged. Even without the parade of naked butts, boobs and variegated bits, it's lurid stuff.

Various locations
neonnaked.com

15

GOD'S OWN JUNKYARD

Glowing gallery of neon signage

Little prepares you for the technicolour panoply of God's Own Junkyard, Walthamstow's temple to neon – every spare inch is covered with intricate glass signs in eye-scraping hues. It was the long-time workshop of pioneering neon artist Chris Bracey: creator of much of seedy Soho's iconic sex-shop branding ('Sodom and Gomorrah mixed with art,' is how he described his craft), as well as props for films like *Eyes Wide Shut* and *Blade Runner*. When he died in 2014, his sons Marcus and Matthew inherited the family trade and the radiant repository itself. You can buy or hire the signs themselves, but there's also an in-house cafe–bar for boozy libations and snacks (for when your eyes need a rest).

Unit 12, Ravenswood Industrial Estate,
Shernhall Street, E17 9HQ
Nearest station: Walthamstow Central
godsownjunkyard.co.uk

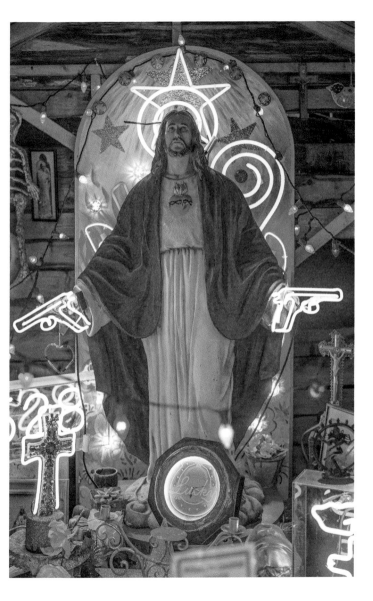

16

VIKTOR WYND MUSEUM OF CURIOSITIES

Wilfully nauseating curiosity cabinet

Horrorshow hoard of a fevered mind? Or an artful homage to the Renaissance *wunderkammer*? This over-stuffed basement museum set beneath a goth absinthe bar is the life's work of the eponymous, enigmatic Wynd, an old-school collector of the esoteric, extreme and plain sickening. Come to ogle the gilded skull of Pablo Escobar's pet hippo and phantasmagoric displays of taxidermy, a putrefying 'Paul Robeson and Pamela Anderson Unification cake', retro porn literature, dusty tribal artefacts from Papua New Guinea and an explicit shrine to the late Soho mega-dandy/arch-shagger Sebastian Horsley. There's something for everyone (though maybe not children).

11 Mare Street, Cambridge Heath Road, E8 4RP
Nearest station: Cambridge Heath
thelasttuesdaysociety.org/museum

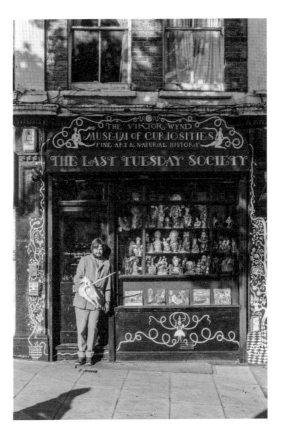

17

DENNIS SEVERS' HOUSE

Timewarp of a Huguenot household

The red-shuttered, artfully-dilapidated frontage of 18 Folgate Street – built in 1724 – conceals a domestic dreamscape unlike any other in London. In 1979, it was bought by Dennis Severs, a Californian emigré who moved to Folgate with a 'candle, a chamber pot and a bedroll' and who, over the next two decades, set about reconceiving the space as the home of an imagined family of Huguenot silk weavers (as you do). Severs created an astounding, living diorama replete with immaculate artwork, household paraphernalia and the tangible trappings of everyday life, laid out in painterly detail and lit to create IRL chiaroscuros worthy of Vermeer (especially apparent on atmospheric evening tours).

18 Folgate Street, E1 6BX
Nearest station: Liverpool Street
dennissevershouse.co.uk

18

LADY DINAH'S CAT EMPORIUM

Feline-filled cafe with a charitable remit

Pet cafes occupy a slightly uncomfortable place in the novelty-cute pantheon – undoubtedly sweet, but all the manhandling a possible cause of animal anxiety. There's no such stress at Lady Dinah's, a Bethnal Green spot modelled on the animal cafes of Japan but with an actively charitable remit. The fantastical Basement Forest, a sylvan subterranea filled with twinkling leaves and gnarled trunks, is a *purrfect* place to settle in for a vegan plate, but the cafe is also a working foster home for the 'clowder' of cats, set up to socialise and, eventually, rehouse its feline wards. More than 60 have gone to permanent homes over the years, making it a truly benevolent little stop-in.

152–154, Bethnal Green Road, E2 6DG
Nearest station: Shoreditch High Street
ladydinahs.com

19

LONGPLAYER

Millennium-long rumination on sound and time

Ambient and drone music tend towards lengthy run times, but Longplayer drags things into the realm of the ridiculous. Created by artist Jem Finer and situated within a 19th-century lighthouse on Trinity Buoy Wharf, this sonorous sound installation began playing on 31 December 1999, and isn't programmed to reset until the same date in 2999. It's a beautiful work – icy, atonal layers drifting like glacial tides, punctuated with metallic clangs – and truly linear, its six constituent pieces forensically calculated to overlap and counterpoint each other without a second of repetition. Too placid? There's also an installation of 234 Tibetan singing bowls – the kind used to created the music in the first place. Zone in.

Trinity Buoy Wharf, 64 Orchard Place, E14 0JW
Nearest station: Canning Town
longplayer.org

20

THE GRAPES

Bellowing actors and watery murder

Best known for being co-owned by uber-thesp Ian McKellan, who occasionally appears in his slippers to host the Monday night quiz, The Grapes is riven with historical clout. It's directly above the spot from which Sir Walter Raleigh set off to the New World, and opaquely mentioned in Dickens's *Our Mutual Friend* (Charles, the exhibitionist, is also said to have danced a jig on the tables). There's also the rumour that local ferry operators would bolster their meagre wages by selling the corpses that bobbed up in the Thames – sometimes creating their own stock by pushing pissed-up Grapes patrons into the water to drown. Today, come for the reliable pints, excellent chips and warm old-world vibe.

76 Narrow Street, E14 8BP
Nearest stations: Wapping, Limehouse
thegrapes.co.uk

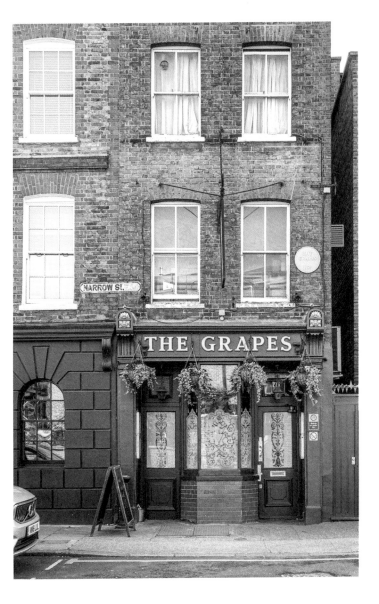

21
DONLON BOOKS

Cool countercultural trove

This fine resource for leftfield publishing was opened by Conor Donlon (former assistant to photography godhead Wolfgang Tillmans) in 2009. It's since become an invaluable (if compact) repository of rare and underground reading material, taking in fringe art, avant-garde architecture and design, esoteric music, photography monographs, erotica, psychedelic drugs, social theory and so on. Eyeball the latest releases from Strange Attractor and Café Royal Books, as well as indie rags like experimental writing platform *Worms*, the perennially horny gay zine *Butt*, neo-antiquarian gem *Weird Walk* and hundreds more. The perfect venue, basically, to grab your mum those books on Japanese noise, auto-trepanning and queer witchcraft she's always coveted.

75 Broadway Market, E8 4PH
Nearest station: London Fields
donlonbooks.com

22

LONDON
FORTEAN SOCIETY

Recherché lectures in a backstreet tavern

Charles Fort (1874–1932, see right) was an American writer and researcher, whose non-dogmatic approach to esoteric phenomena – the paranormal, UFOs, alchemy, folklore, cryptozoology, pseudoscience and more – gave us the term 'Fortean'. Today, David Barrett and Scott Wood channel Fort's application of humanity and humour to these topics via their London Fortean Society talks, normally held at The Bell. The scope is broad – expect anything from medieval church graffiti and Cumberland's 'Croglin Grange' vampire, to a history of execution postcards, cursed ornamental cabinets and the occult art of the Tate Britain archive. As gloriously hokey as it is deeply informative.

The Bell, 50 Middlesex Street, E1 7EX
Nearest station: Aldgate East
forteanlondon.blogspot.com

23

THE TEN BELLS

Pints, poltergeists and Ripper yarns

Plenty of London's pubs claim to be the city's most jinxed, but The Ten Bells – a thronging boozer beside Hawksmoor's Christ Church Spitalfields – has cred both spectral *and* grimly corporeal. Workers in the 1990s tell of feeling the phantasmal form of Victorian landlord George Roberts ambling the upper floors (and, occasionally, shuffling into bed with overnighting bar staff), while whispers of a murdered baby have given even hardened psychics the willies. The Ripper stuff is grimmer still: Jack's second victim – Annie Chapman – was found mutilated in a yard off nearby Hanbury Street on 8 November 1888 after drinking at the Bells, and her presence is said to persist in poltergeist form.

84 Commercial Street, E1 6LY
Nearest station: Liverpool Street
tenbells.com

24

FATBERG MEMORIAL MANHOLE COVER

Recessed remembrance to an odious icon

Ah, the London fatberg boom: hazy, halcyon days across the 2010s, when truly disgusting compounds of fat, oil and grease (congealed with condoms, face wipes and other idly flushed detritus) threatened to block the city's antiquated sewer networks. Unfortunate workers (or 'flushers') embraced the task of water-blasting, hacking and sawing the nauseating masses to bits. They were always big – one discovered in Kingston was the size of a bus – but the whopper unearthed in Whitechapel in 2017, a colossal 250 metres long and 130 tonnes in weight, was beyond the pale. Those looking to pay their respects to the stinky superstar should head outside Whitechapel tube, where Thames Water has installed a commemorative plate to its defeated adversary.

The manhole can be found right of the station exit,
where Court Street and Whitechapel Road meet, E1 2BB
Nearest station: Whitechapel

25

EXECUTION DOCK

End of the road for damned pirates

They may look inauspicious today, but Wapping Old Stairs – a narrow passageway along the side of the Town of Ramsgate pub, leading down to the murky Thames foreshore – once heralded one of the grisliest locales in London: Execution Dock. From the 15th century until 1830, a waterside gibbet (positioned into the river, where the admiralty's rule of law commenced) was used to string up errant pirates, mutineers and other naughty nautical types, who would be left in situ until three tides had raised over their lifeless bodies. The gallows are long gone, but a macabre replica sits outside the Prospect of Whitby to the east, next to Shadwell Basin.

Wapping Old Stairs, next to the Town of Ramsgate,
62 Wapping High Street, E1W 2PN
The replica dock: 57 Wapping Wall, E1W 3SH
Nearest station: Wapping

26

CROSSBONES GRAVEYARD

Artistic memorial for outcast dead

A fence festooned with ribbons, hand-written dedications, flowers and trinkets marks your arrival at Crossbones, a former pauper's cemetery located in what was once a violent slum. This is the burial site for the Winchester Geese (a cohort of medieval sex workers licensed by the Bishop of Winchester) and 15,000 other 'outcast dead'. Rediscovered in 1996 by local writer John Constable (allegedly via a visitation from the spirit of a sex worker) and transformed over two subsequent decades into an extant sanctuary, it is dotted with shrines, a sinuous wooden cloister, an oyster-shell-covered pyramid, wildflowers and a syphilitic skull replica. An atmospheric vigil to its unfortunate denizens is still held on the 23rd of every month.

Union Street, SE1 1TA
Nearest station: London Bridge
crossbones.org.uk

27

THE CLINK

Delectable dinner at His Majesty's pleasure

Once a temporary digs for Mick Jagger, Bertrand Russell, local rapper Giggs and Glenn Danzig of the Misfits, HMP Brixton isn't an obvious venue for a refined dinner. But lo: The Clink is a nifty, charity-run restaurant, staffed by prisoners training for catering qualifications and located in the old governor's house. There's a militant rigmarole: no booze, a pre-dinner security briefing and a long list of banned items (including phones, umbrellas, hats and, er, tissues). The menu, redolent of any number of bijous London joints, is a lyrical, seasonal treat: confit leek and cheddar gougeres; hen of the woods with Jerusalem artichoke and truffle jus; braised venison ragu ravioli; et al. The secret ingredient... is crime.

HMP Brixton, Jebb Avenue, SW2 5XF
Nearest station: Brixton
theclinkcharity.org/restaurants/brixton

28

CONTROL ROOM B

Retro-futurist mixology in Battersea Power Station

This whizz-bang cocktail bar is found deep inside Giles Gilbert Scott's magnificent Battersea Power Station, in its former electricity control centre. It's a singular spot: the Art-Deco-goes-steampunk visuals are wonderfully conceived, and the original 1950s panels, synchroscopes, switchgear and energy dials kept intact for full space-age appeal. An optional audio tour provides granular immersion into its buzzing history and, naturally, there's an incorporated 'Escape the Power Cut' game for people who demand organised fun with their booze. And yes, space-rock stans, those *are* the decks from the cover of Hawkwind's mid-tier 1977 album, *Quark, Strangeness and Charm*. Cosmic stuff.

Battersea Power Station, Circus Road West, SW11 8BZ
Nearest station: Battersea Power Station
controlroomb.com

29

SYDENHAM HILL WOOD

Occult woodland rites and a sinister shaft

An otherwise tranquil haven from the clamour of south London, Sydenham Hill Wood boasts two disquieting features. First, the Victorian folly of a ruined gothic chapel, now a site of odd nocturnal rites (walkers having found pigs' heads and lit candles on its tumbled stonework). Then, the boarded entrance of the Paxton Tunnel, built in 1852 to connect Nunhead and Crystal Palace by rail. Peeking into its shadowy depths is creepy as is – but eerier still when bolstered by a tale of a runner falling into the shaft through loose earth, only to find a carriage full of skeletons in period dress, abandoned to their fate when the line was shuttered in the 1950s...

63 Crescent Wood Road, SE26 6SA
Nearest station: Sydenham Hill

30

CRYSTAL PALACE DINOSAURS

Anatomically awry monsters

Of all Crystal Palace Park's curios – the rusted Corten concert stage and two recumbent Sphinx statues among them – none are as cartoonishly fearsome as the 30 dinosaurs that loom over the park's southern lake. Created by the natural history illustrator Benjamin Waterhouse Hawkins between 1853–55, they were given a much-needed spruce in 2017. 'Dinosaur' is actually a misnomer of a catch-all that includes reptiles, amphibians, pterodactyls and other mega-fauna – the maniacally staring ichthyosaur, a giant ground sloth making moves on a tree trunk and two hulking iguanodons (bearing zero resemblance to their true cretaceous counterparts) are particular standouts.

Thicket Road, SE20
Nearest station: Penge West
cpdinosaurs.org

31

STRAWBERRY HILL HOUSE

Ornate ersatz castle and home of Gothic literature

The battlements, lancet windows, carved beasts on the stairs, mock-medieval detailing and painterly 'contrivances' (including a garden bench in the shape of a giant Rococo shell) give this Twickenham castle – the former seat of 18th-century writer Horace Walpole – a hardcore fairy-tale vibe. But a more unearthly subtext lingers. Walpole bought the estate in 1747, spending decades overhauling it into a mad toybox villa and prompting a frenzied Gothic Revival in the process. Feel a room-chilling darkness? You're not alone. Walpole suffered a night-terror vision of an armoured hand on the banister and was inspired to write his pioneering medievalist horror novel *The Castle of Otranto* as a result. Made his own bed, frankly.

268 Waldegrave Road, Twickenham, TW1 4ST
Nearest station: Strawberry Hill
strawberryhillhouse.org.uk

32
MUDLARKING WALKS

Half-buried treasures on the river's foreshore

Given the Thames' historically rich and palpably murky history, an unfathomable amount of crap has been lost to its opaque waters. Its banks were fertile places for 18th- and 19th-century scavengers – or 'mudlarks' – who would scour the grimy sands for items of scant value. The profession is kaput, but mudlarking as a pastime persists. The Thames' sludge proffers a kaleidoscope of cool artefacts: Elizabethan clay pipes, pewter toys, Medieval pilgrim and secular badges, buckles, broaches, buttons, dice, bits of bone and bottles among 'em. It's regulated these days – requiring permits and formal declaration of finds – so partake in a Thames Explore Trust's guided 'lark around Wapping or Rotherhithe. Don't take anything home, and for god's sake wash your hands afterwards.

Various locations
thames-explorer.org.uk/guided-tours

33

CATACOMBS AT WEST NORWOOD CEMETERY

Crumbling coffins beneath a Gothic graveyard

Perhaps the Magnificent Seven cemeteries' most underrated member – without the enveloping foliage and celeb fripperies of the others, but with the distinction of being the world's first Gothic Revival graveyard – West Norwood's most horrendous attraction lies in its crumbling catacombs. Consecrated in 1837, they're a gloomy warren of 95 private vaults and communal enclaves (around 3,500 all in). Many of the coffins are decaying to dust, so that their occupants – the latest of which was laid down in the 1930s – are allegedly visible through the holes. Respect for the dead (and, presumably, hygiene) means they're only periodically accessible to the living, via tours run by the Friends of West Norwood Cemetery.

Norwood Road, SE27 9JU
Nearest station: West Norwood
fownc.org

34
CHISLEHURST CAVES

A labyrinthine system beneath suburban Bromley

In 1903, it was claimed that this outer-London tangle of tunnels and caverns had been dug out by the Romans, Saxons and Druids (who used them for pagan rituals), while anthropologist Sir Arthur Keith deemed them a more significant work of prehistoric labour than Avebury's ceremonial megaliths. All claptrap. Chislehurst's 22 miles of passageways were carved from the 13th century onwards to mine chalk and flint, but they *have* since hosted a mushroom farm, WWII shelter, damp music venue (Bowie played here four times, Hendrix twice) and setting for the 1988 video to Iron Maiden's walloping 'Can I Play With Madness?'. Today, the caves' rich history is brought to vivid and unnerving life by a cast of mannequins, illuminated by kerosene lamps on guided tours of the labyrinth.

Caveside Close, Old Hill, Chislehurst, BR7 5NL
Nearest station: Chislehurst
chislehurst-caves.co.uk

35

HOUSE OF DREAMS

Vividly moving tribute to love and lives lost

There can't be many installations as alluringly immersive, compelling and sincere as outsider artist–designer Stephen Wright's House of Dreams. The project kicked off in 1999 as an ever-permuting diary of Wright's life ('and former lives') stemming from the loss of his late partner and parents. It's near impossible to evoke in totality, but expect hyper-intricate grotto-style walls, pictorial tiling and floor mosaics; bits of chichi Catholic ephemera and south Asian shrines; surreal anthropomorphic 'comfort sculptures' incorporating his father's false teeth and mother's dresses; and hundreds of mouldering toy dolls, bottle tops, hair-rollers, vinyl records and reams of Delphic text art. As living artworks go, it's melancholy and, in its own idiosyncratic way, really rather beautiful.

45 Melbourne Grove, SE22 8RG
Nearest station: East Dulwich
stephenwrightartist.com/house-of-dreams

36
LONDON LOO TOURS

Go down the bend into London's latrine history

Eschewing the tour-guide's flag for a (squeaky clean) plunger, lav-loving Rachel Cole-Wilkin has been leading these guides to the city's outhouses for over a decade. Originally spurred by an obsession with finding places to pee for free, the tours morphed into 90-minute ambles around the city's public conveniences. Rachel discusses everything from the legacy of Thomas Crapper and how the Romans did their business, to right-on discussions around gender equality and accessibility, by way of pop-up urinals, in-construction super sewers, London's slimmest alleyway (not a loo, but grimly adjacent), the city's priciest public john and, the big draw, London's most patriotic toilet: the South Bank Jubiloo, opened to mark Queen Elizabeth II's Diamond Jubilee.

Most tours start from outside the public toilets at
Waterloo Station, SE1 8SR
lootours.com

37
CROWNED STINKPIPE

Lofty Victorian vent with a regal twist

Blink and you'll miss them, but like mice on a Tube track, London's 'stinkpipes' become increasingly ubiquitous when you know where to look. They're akin to towering lampposts without the lamp (sometimes green, sometimes grey), installed to vent fetid air out of the sewer system that was built by Joseph Bazalgette after Victorian London's Great Stink of 1858 (a long, hot summer when the scatological build-up in the Thames began to ferment). Many of them are vaguely embellished with decorations, but none are as comely as the one on Kennington Cross – a totemic grey pedestal, column and pole, topped with a burnished gold crown.

Kennington Cross is at the intersection of Kennington Road, Kennington Lane and Cleaver Street, SE11 4EZ
Nearest station: Kennington

38
SEVEN NOSES OF SOHO

Artsy septet of anti-authoritarian beaks

In 1997, aggrieved at the proliferation of Orwellian surveillance around London, Rick Buckley did what any other mischievous, Situationist-inspired artist would do in protest: he covertly stuck 35 plaster casts of his own hooter to alfresco surfaces around town (all in the sight of CCTV and painted to blend, chameleon like, into their surroundings). Most were removed by 'the man', but seven remain; the most famous of which – half-way up the wall at Admiralty Arch, off Trafalgar Square – isn't in Soho at all (and sometimes erroneously thought to have been moulded on Napoleon's; or that it's a spare schnozz for Nelson). A bit of cursory Googling will find you the rest.

Nearest stations: Piccadilly Circus, Leicester Square, Tottenham Court Road

39

ATTENDANT COFFEE ROASTERS

An oat flat white in an underground pissoir?

This micro-chain and roastery is one of the capital's finest purveyors of speciality coffee. In a sea of shops awash in soaped woods and Brutalist geometrics, its Fitzrovia branch offers a cool USP, housed in a (mercifully) repurposed public men's loo dating from 1890 and flush with neat contemporary details. Settle in with a perfectly extracted espresso and admire the dormant cisterns, shiny white tiling and undulating porcelain of the former urinals – now a counter of stalls where you can while away the day, feet in the one-time drain.

27a Foley Street, W1W 6DY
Nearest stations: Oxford Circus, Goodge Street
the-attendant.com

40

HORIZON EDIBLE INSECTS

The future of food in an Ealing shed

Relentless are the effusive broadsheet reports on how we all should be eating insects as a sustainable form of protein. Ground zero for London's edible arthropod movement is Horizon, an insect farm in the back garden of an innocuous west London home. After a brief tour of the farm, head into the kitchen to learn how to make cricket-topped bruschetta, insect nuggets and 'crispy chocolate mealworm cupcakes', among other antennae-laced morsels. They also sell take-home products like edible locusts (mildly meaty and a perfect 'starter bug'), grow-your-own mealworm kits and 'frass' (insect dung, a great fertiliser). Ethically sound, environmentally astute and bizarrely delicious? That's the joy of 'sects.

9 Queen Anne's Grove, W5 3XP
Nearest station: South Ealing
horizoninsects.co.uk

41

THE TIROLER HUT

Cowbell-chorused Austrian plates

London's mid-century food scene is not generally considered a feted era. Thank god, though, that The Tiroler Hut – an Austro-Alpine basement restaurant, opened in 1967 by Josef Friedmann – prevails. Amble down the clackety staircase into a place from another time: red-and-white chequered tablecloths; chalet panelling; straining lederhosen; dulcet yodelling; and, most totemic of all, Josef (the 'Bavarian Sinatra', quoth *Time Out*) leading knie-hoch singalongs, before cracking out his symphonious star attractions: the cowbells (plural). A sea of apricot schnapps, jugs of foaming Märzen beer and plates of artery-furring fondue, schnitzel, spätzle and käsekrainer complete the jolly scene. *Prost*!

27 Westbourne Grove, W2 4UA
Nearest stations: Bayswater and Royal Oak
tirolerhutrestaurant.co.uk

42

ELFIN OAK

Fairy kingdom carved into an ancient oak

After being moved from Richmond Park to Kensington Gardens in 1928, this pollarded oak was set upon by the Cornish children's book illustrator and woodcarver Ivor Innes. He reimagined its gnarled levels as an intricate world of Technicolour faerie-folk, woodsy fauna, melancholy harlequins, gnomes, imps and smoking elves – all of whom were given magical backstories by his wife Elsie Innes in her 1930 book *The Elfin Oak of Kensington Gardens*. A fantastical panoply, the tree's whimsical value was recognised by comedian Spike Milligan in the 1960s, who funded the restoration of the then-deteriorating trunk.

Next to the Princess Diana Children's Playground,
Broad Walk, Kensington Palace Gardens, W2 4RU
Nearest station: Queensway
royalparks.org.uk/visit/parks/kensington-gardens

43

GRAVE OF
GIRO THE DOG

Dinky dedication to a fascist Fido

The UK's sole monument to a Nazi isn't quite as deplorable as it sounds. Giro was a terrier owned by one-time German ambassador (and popular local socialite) Leopold von Hoesch. He came to Britain as a servant of the Weimar Republic in 1932, but his (and Giro's) allegiances segued to Hitler a year later by default. In 1934, the scrappy furball chewed through a cable in the garden of the embassy at 9 Carlton House, died of electrocution and was subsequently (after an unconfirmed burial with full Nazi pageantry) memorialised with a tiny headstone. It's now in a perspex-fronted case in front of a tree just off the Mall.

9 Carlton Terrace, SW1Y 5AG
Nearest station: Piccadilly Circus

44

TOMB OF HANNAH COURTOY

A hidden time machine in an Egypt-themed tomb

Brompton Cemetery is awash with esoteric symbology, but little pips the tomb of Hannah Courtoy (d. 1849) – a faux-Egyptian mausoleum that, er, houses a working time machine. It was designed by inventor Samuel Alfred Warner and Egyptologist Joseph Bonomi, who apparently decoded the secrets of interdimensional travel from hieroglyphics found on an expedition. Together, they built a time machine, hiding it in this megalithic box (Courtoy, it's said, funded the endeavour). Bonomi is buried nearby but Warner disappeared, perhaps zipping off into the folds of time himself. Naturally, the key to the tomb is long lost.

Courtoy's tomb is located on the east side of the cemetery
Fulham Road, SW10 9UG
Nearest station: West Brompton
royalparks.org.uk/visit/parks/brompton-cemetery

45

MORPETH ARMS

Bankside boozer with a haunted basement

Built in 1845 for the wardens of Millbank Prison, the Morpeth Arms sits over a warren of cells and tunnels, from which doomed convicts would be led for deportation to Australia. One died attempting an escape and his spirit is now said to haunt the pub, with staff reporting low-key poltergeist activity and a weird, icy atmosphere – so much so that they've installed a video link from the basement to the bar, so punters can keep an eye out for spectres while supping a London Best. Spooks abound upstairs too: the 'Spying Room' has a fine aspect of MI6 across the river, complete with binoculars for peering into the Security Service's jade-coloured windows.

58 Millbank, SW1P 4RW
Nearest station: Pimlico
morpetharms.com

46

THE COSMIC HOUSE

Postmodernist home in rarefied west London

The *Grand Designs* that never was, late American landscape designer Charles Jencks' Cosmic House is a postmodern palimpsest that makes tangible his wild ideas around art, architecture, cosmology, symbolism and myth. The place is truly bananas: from the inverted stucco facade, to a malachite-floored gallery with concrete poetry friezes decorating the walls; a cylindrical staircase referencing the helix forms of time and space; an ochre hearth filled with Chinese 'scholar's rocks', topped with a bust of Hephaestus (with Pop Art pioneer Eduardo Paolozzi's face); a jacuzzi bathtub in the form of an upended Borromini cupola; dummy doors and neo-Hellenistic furnishings; and a topiary-filled 'Time Garden'. That's scratching the surface; McCloud would have *flipped*.

19 Lansdowne Walk, W11 3AH
Nearest station: Holland Park
jencksfoundation.org/cosmic-house

47

THE LANGHAM

A full cast of ghosts at a five-star hotel

One of London's most classically bijous hotels is also its most spectre-crammed. Where to start? Back in 1973, a BBC newscaster claimed they saw a ghostly orb of light take the form of a legless (literally; not drunk) Victorian man in room 333 – still the building's most frequently reported spooker. There's a phantasmic butler on the third floor. A German prince in military garb by the fourth-floor window from which he leapt in the early 1900s. The ghost of former French president Napoleon III in the basement (why not?). And, best of all, some seismic poltergeist activity that freaked out a decent raft of the 2014 English test cricket team, Stuart Broad and Ben Stokes among them. *Howzat* for hair-raising?

1c Portland Place, W1B 1JA
Nearest station: Oxford Circus
langhamhotels.com

48

THE CHURCHILL ARMS

Ostentatiously floral facade on a patriotic pub

Most rarefied London pubs boast a hanging basket
or two on their frontage, but the florid lunacy of
this Notting Hill pile would give the most ardent
Chelsea Flower Show fan paroxysms. The Churchill Arms – built in 1750, the bar famously propped
up by Winston Churchill's grandparents, the pub
then renamed after the Third Reich's trouncing in
'45 – boasts a fragrant 100 pots, 42 baskets and 48
window boxes across its exterior, all maintained at
a cool cost of more than £26,000 per year. Inside,
there's a supplementary sea of Winston mem-
orabilia and a decent Thai kitchen. Borderline
jingoistic? Maybe. Indubitably fetching? Absolutely.
Hayfever sufferers should take a wide berth.

119 Kensington Church Street, W8 7LN
Nearest station: Notting Hill Gate
churchillarmskensington.co.uk

49

FITZROVIA CHAPEL

A golden sanctuary in new-build hell

Plonked incongruously in the soul-sinking Pearson Square development, the Fitzrovia Chapel's sheeny exterior and uncannily perfect lawn might look synthetic – but the interior of this red-brick pile is beatific beyond belief. Designed in 1891 by John Loughborough Pearson and completed in the 1930s by his son Frank, the space comprises a series of flamboyant mosaics: from the baptistry ceiling's cerulean wash and looming seraphs, set above a green marble font inscribed with the palindrome *Nipson anomēmata mē monan opsin* ('Wash the sins and not only my face'); to the star-speckled gold firmament of the main nave; and the relatively subdued (but still lavish) Romanesque floors. It's God's gift to Fitzrovia.

2 Pearson Square, W1T 3BF
Nearest station: Goodge Street
fitzroviachapel.org

50

HYDE PARK PET CEMETERY

Final resting place for beloved companions

In the northern reaches of Hyde Park, visible through iron railings around the gatekeeper's cottage of Victoria Lodge, is one of London's most sweetly heartbreaking locales. This overgrown lot, filled with miniature marble headstones, was, in the late 1800s, a modish final resting place for over 1,000 aristocratic pets. George Orwell, the curmudgeon, decried it as 'perhaps the most horrible spectacle in Britain' – reason enough to take a snoop – but it's a haunting, mournful place, the most elegiac dedication within which reads: 'Here lie two faithful creatures / Snap and Peter / We are only sleeping, master.' (No, *you* have something in your eye.) It's only accessible to the public via dedicated Royal Parks tours.

41 Bayswater Road, W2 4RQ
Nearest station: Lancaster Gate
royalparks.org.uk/news-blogs-press-releases/
hyde-park-pet-cemetery

51

BROAD STREET CHOLERA PUMP

Strangely sanitised memorial to a grim disease

On 31 August 1854, an outbreak of cholera hit Soho. Within two weeks, three-quarters of the overcrowded, poorly sanitised district's populace had fled and over 500 people had keeled. The heroic physician John Snow pinned the epidemic not on miasmic air, but foul water taken from a public pump on Broad (now Broadwick) Street, which was duly disabled, stymying the spread. Since 1993, the John Snow Society has held an annual 'Pump-handle Lecture' at Bloomsbury's London School of Hygiene and Tropical Medicine. Culminating in the ceremonial removal of the original pump's handle, attendees then traipse to Broadwick Street for ritual tipples at the John Snow pub, overlooking this disease-free replica.

Outside the John Snow, 39 Broadwick Street, W1F 9QJ
Nearest stations: Oxford Circus, Piccadilly Circus

52

HOXTON STREET MONSTER SUPPLIES

Dispensary of grotesque and ghastly groceries

This ghoulish provisioner of 'bespoke and every-day items for the living, dead and undead' is operated by the Ministry of Stories – a charity set up by Nick Hornby to encourage creative writing in young people. It's all beautifully realised; the interior a winsomely uncanny facsimile of an antiquated post-office/apothecary, shelves heaving with soap-encased cockroaches, 'Vague Sense of Unease' humbugs, smoky 'London Smog' flavour drops, 'Thickest Human Snot' (lemon curd), chocolate brains under glass cloches, salt made from 'the Tears of Home Schooling' and other disgustingly delectable titbits. But take note: 'Customers,' pleads the pithy window signage, 'are politely requested to refrain from eating the staff.'

159 Hoxton Street, N1 6PJ
Nearest station: Hoxton
monstersupplies.org

53

PARKLAND
WALK SPRIGGAN

A spooky sprite

Trot along Parkland Walk – the remnant of a railway line that once ran from Alexandra Palace to Finsbury Park, now a bucolic byway – and glance upwards at the old brick arches just before Crouch Hill station. Peering back, you'll see something rather eldritch: the Spriggan. An amalgam of Pan and a gnarled old sprite, this dreamlike figurehead is a malevolent figure in Cornish history, transposed to cosmopolitan north London by the artist Marilyn Collins in 1993, who designed the sculpture to honour Crouch End's fertile history of permaculture. Clambering from its archway, the spooky sentinel remains incongruous – no surprise it was an apocryphal inspiration for Stephen King's short story 'Crouch End'.

The closest access to the Spriggan is from
Vicarage Path, near Crouch End Hill Bridge
off Crouch Hill Road, N4 4SE
Nearest station: Crouch Hill

54

HIGHGATE CEMETERY

London's most storied graveyard

Opened in 1839, London's pre-eminent cemetery is still a working burial ground, with around 80 people interred each year. It's a beautiful place, the greenery-shrouded west side of which holds particularly enigmatic appeal, with its obelisk-guarded Egyptian avenue, tomb-circled Cedar of Lebanon and terrace catacombs (plus the grave of George Michael). Highgate's ghostly history, too, is intriguing: whether reports of a lady hovering above a pond, *The Innocents*-style, or an ethereal cyclist pedalling about. Weirder still was the 1970s panic that sprung up around the Highgate Vampire: a demonic being that was said to prowl the grounds, causing a stand-off between two press-hungry occult investigators and exorcists. Visitors, remember: respect for the grieving is paramount.

Swain's Lane, N6 6PJ
Nearest station: Archway
highgatecemetery.org

55

CYBERDOG

Luminescent pioneer of future-rave fashions

A throwback to '90s Camden in the otherwise
unbearable, tourist-heaving sprawl of the Stables
Market, Cyberdog is an emporium of eye-peeling
rave, neo-goth, cybertronic, techno streetwear and
fetish gear, visually inescapable for the whacking-
great chrome cyborgs that flank the door. Inside,
things are just as outré, with neon plastic colon-
nades, UV lighting, gyrating podium dancers and
a hoofing 4/4 soundtrack. An evergreen presence
since its origins as a stall in 1994 (before shift-
ing into a series of tunnels below the market, and
then into its current home), the vibe is both nos-
talgic and – as the tides of fashion turn and the
Y2K aesthetic comes in vogue again – increasingly,
inexplicably hip.

The Stables Market, Chalk Farm Road, NW1 8AH
Nearest stations: Camden Town, Chalk Farm
cyberdog.net

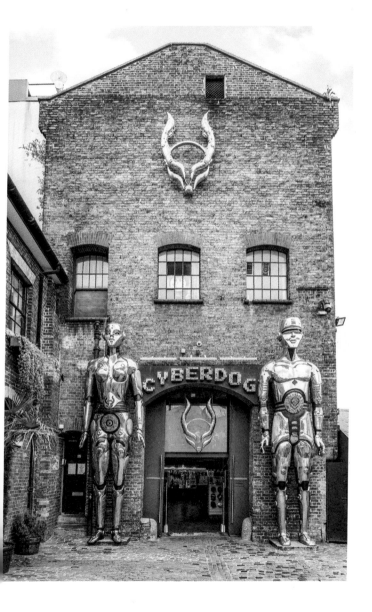

56

TAXIDERMY AT PARK AVENUE STUDIOS

Rodent dioramas in a garden workshop

Get a feel for nature at one of Suzette Field's viscerally enlightening taxidermy days, run from her studio in Crouch End. She's been guiding the public in stuffing a peaceable kingdom of furry, feathered and winged things for over a decade, though her workshops tend to focus on rodents. These are carefully 'degloved' of their skins, which are then cleaned and treated, before being re-laid over a clay head and wire body and mounted into anthropomorphic scenes with dinky outfits and props. Other animals – crows, cockerels, weasels et al – and more fiendish 'rogues' (two-headed or winged rats) are available on request, and lunch (vegan, naturally) is included.

22 Park Avenue South, N8 8LT
Nearest stations: Highgate, Hornsey
afieldguide.org/workshops.html

57

KING'S CROSS
ICE WELL

Temple to deep freezing

The subdued appellation of the London Canal Museum's 'ice well' doesn't prepare you for the grandiose size and eeriness of the thing itself: a four-metre-deep chasm lit in Picton blue hues. Built in the 1850s, it was used to store giant blocks of ice imported from Norwegian mountain lakes. The whole chilly shebang was established by Swiss entrepreneur Carlo Gatti, a wildly bearded visionary who also introduced ice cream to the UK (hence the provision of sweet gelato ephemera nearby). You can generally only peer down into the depths, but there's rare public access on the special Ice Well Sunday in July, and at Christmas a choir is sent in to exploit the well's haunting acoustics.

12/13 New Wharf Road, N1 9RT
Nearest station: King's Cross St Pancras
canalmuseum.org.uk/ice/ice-wells

58

OSLO COURT

Toothsome timewarp in a retro Regent's Park block

On the ground floor of the eponymous, 1930s International Modern-style housing block, Oslo Court is a soft-focus French restaurant from another era. Specifically, from 1982: a year – with its cruise-ship table settings, silver service, floral drapes and bygone menus – it remains steadfastly entrenched within. Having enjoyed something of a renaissance, dewy-eyed London fooderati now traipse again to St John's Wood for whimsical plates of pastry-encased crab à la Rochelle, lobster cocktails swimming in Marie-Rose, melon with Parma ham, crispy duck à l'orange and sole meunière. All capped off, crucially, with the heaving house dessert trolley: professional dominion of twinkly-eyed pudding potentate Neil Heshmat – London's most adored and probably longest-serving waiter.

Charlbert Street, NW8 7EN
Nearest station: St John's Wood
oslocourtrestaurant.co.uk

59

KAREN'S DINER

Wilfully atrocious service at a retro diner

Crap service is generally seen as a bad thing in hospitality. Not so at Karen's, a 1950s-style diner named in homage to the archetypally obnoxious, meme-adjacent suburban woman. Here, your retro burgers, fries and shakes are served with a side of apoplectic and foul-mouthed backchat by the staff, whose job it is to make sure you have absolutely the worst time possible. Insults range from brusquely profane to impressively personal. Neither adults nor children are spared, and so long as you play within the rules (that is, no body shaming, no slurs), you're allowed (nay, expected) to give as good as you get.

9 White Lion Street, N1 9PD
Nearest station: Angel
bemorekaren.com

IMAGE CREDITS

Intro Section: © Nick Harrison / Alamy; © David Post; © David Post; Roger Garfield / Alamy; © Novelty Automation; © Naked Neon

Main Entries: Novelty Automation (first and third image) © Martin Usborne, second image © Leon Neal / Getty Images; Sarastro © Mjf Studio Photographic Breau; Dans le Noir © Dans Le Noir?; Grant Museum of Zoology © PA Images / Alamy; Jeremy Bentham © Nick Harrison / Alamy; Treadwell's Bookshop © Ellen Christina Hancock; Seven Stars © David Post; Haunted Underground Stations © Joe Dunckley / Alamy; London Ghost Walks © Laura Prieto, courtesy of London Ghost Walks; Hand of Saint Etheldreda © David Post; The Cornhill Devils © Jeffrey Isaac Greenberg 5 + / Alamy; Hunterian Museum © Hufton + Crow, images courtesy Hunterian Museum; Golden Boy of Pye Corner © Angelo Hornak / Alamy; Neon Naked Life Drawing © Neon Naked Life Drawing; God's Own Junkyard © Roger Garfield / Alamy; Viktor Wynd Museum of Curiosities © Oskar Proctor, images courtesy Viktor Wynd Museum; Dennis Severs' House © Charlotte Schreiber; Lady Dinah's Cat Emporium © David Post; London Player first image © Nathaniel Noir / Alamy, second image © James Whitaker; The Grapes © Tim George; Donlon Books © Charlotte Schreiber; The Ten Bells © Tim George; Fatberg Memorial Manhole Cover © Andy Scott; Execution Dock © Tim George; Crossbones Graveyard © Paula French / Alamy; The Clink © The Clink; Control Room B first image © Johnny Stephens, second image © Tim Atkins; Sydenham Hill Woods © Veronique Stone / Dreamstime.com; Crystal Palace Dinosaurs © Marco Kessler; Strawberry Hill House first image © Ian Dagnall / Alamy, second & third images © Tony French / Alamy; Mudlarking Walks © Alex Ramsay / Alamy; Catacombs at West Norwood Cemetery © Julian Nieman; Chislehurst Caves first image © Paul Hill / Alamy, second image © Kumar Sriskandan / Alamy; House of Dreams © Michael Vaughan courtesy House of Dreams; London Loo Tours © David Post; Crowned Stinkpipe © David Post; The Seven Noses of Soho © Nathaniel Noir / Alamy; Attendant Coffee © Nathaniel Noir / Alamy; Horizon Edible Insects © Andia / Alamy; Tiroler Hut © David Post; Elfin Oak © Mark Phillips / Alamy; Grave of Giro the Dog © Graham Bridgeman-Clarke / Alamy; The Tomb of Hannah Courtoy © Juliet Ferguson / Alamy; Morpeth Arms © Kumar Sriskandan / Alamy; The Cosmic House © Sue Barr, images courtesy The Cosmic House; The Langham Hotel © The Langham, London; The Churchill Arms © Mike Clegg / Alamy; Fitzrovia Chapel first two images © Hufton + Crow-VIEW / Alamy, third image © Frederick Wood – Punchy / Alamy; Hyde Park Pet Cemetery © Panther Media GmbH / Alamy; Broad Street Cholera Pump © David Post; Hoxton Street Monster Supplies © Lesley Lau; Parkland Walk Spriggan © John Michaels / Alamy; Highgate Cemetry © Taran Wilkhu; Cyperdog © agsaz / alamy; Taxidermy at Park Avenue Studios © Taxidermy at Park Avenue Studios; King's Cross Ice Well © David Post; Oslo Court © David Post; Karen's Diner © Jeff Gilbert / Alamy

Many thanks to Ruby, Dulcie, Ally, Fred, Andrew, Sujata, Rosie and Lydia who, more than most, had to suffer the endless wittering and gallivanting that would eventually become this book. Thanks, too, to Flo, Martin and Ann at Hoxton Mini Press for tolerating my whims and buckling to the fatberg.

*An Opinionated Guide
to Weird London*
First edition

Published in 2024
by Hoxton Mini Press, London
Copyright © Hoxton Mini Press 2024.
All rights reserved.

Text by Tom Howells
Editing by Florence Ward
Design and production
by Richard Mason
Proofreading by Zoë Jellicoe
Editorial support by Leona Crawford

With thanks to Matthew Young for
initial series design.

Please note: we recommend checking the websites listed for each entry before you visit for the latest information on price, opening times and pre-booking requirements.

Thank you to all of the individuals and institutions who have provided images and arranged permissions. While every effort has been made to trace the present copyright holders we apologise in advance for any unintentional omission or error, and would be pleased to insert the appropriate acknowledgement in any subsequent edition.

A CIP catalogue record for this book is available from the British Library.

ISBN: 978-1-914314-68-1

Printed and bound by OZGraf, Poland

Hoxton Mini Press is an environmentally conscious publisher, committed to offsetting our carbon footprint. This book is 100 per cent carbon compensated, with offset purchased from Stand For Trees.

Every time you order from our website, we plant a tree:
www.hoxtonminipress.com

Selected opinionated guides in the series:

For more go to www.hoxtonminipress.com

INDEX